ALMA DE NIÑO

SONGBOOK 1

Yago Santos

Transcriptions from the author's recording, *Alma de Niño*
UPC: 8428353760518

MEL BAY

Cover photo by Diego Gallardo. www.flamencuras.es

Introduction

Alma de Niño (Soul of a Child) is the title of Yago Santos' first album, a deep and introspective work full of character, colors and textures that portray a modern approach to traditional flamenco music and compositional style. The full album consists of fifteen expansive works transcribed by the composer in two volumes entitled *Alma de Niño Songbook 1* and *Alma de Niño Songbook 2*. The solo guitar pieces or *toques* contained in the album represent moments and moods that are reflected in a wide variety of flamenco *palos* or styles, such as *solea por bulerias, tientos, rondeña, bulerias, taranta, solea, guajira,* and *fandango de Huelva*—among others.

Yago's music reflects his unique personality as a flamenco guitarist. Al Di Meola described it as "...brilliant, in a forward-thinking way, extending the vocabulary of this wonderful idiom of music." The music of *Alma de Niño* highlights the lyricis of the melodies, the abundant left-hand slurs, the original arpeggio patterns and the powerful *rajeos* that emphasize the characteristic rhythms of the pieces. His mentor, the renowned flamenco guitarist Rafael Riqueni, described the album as "... timeless work, a step forward in flamenco guitar."

Reflections on *ALMA DE NIÑO SONGBOOK 1*

It is always difficult for composers to talk about their own work without falling into subjective criteria, but in a few words, I will try to describe what *Alma de Niño* means to me and the vivid experiences that have motivated the composition of the pieces on this recording.

I began to consider the composition of *Alma de Niño* back in 2010, shortly after leaving my hometown of Bilbao (Spain), where I acquired my love of music from my mother, who was my first teacher. As a piano aficionado, she instilled in me discipline and good work habits, first on the piano and then on the guitar— values that I have carried with me ever since. It was precisely in 2010 when I began to shape the first piece of this work, "*A Fali*" (To Fali), dedicated to my second teacher, Rafael ("Fali") Riqueni, whom I met in Madrid that same year.

I had already made the first sketches for this *solea por buleria* in Seville a few months earlier, the result of intense afternoon with the guitar in which I tried to describe the magical sunsets and dawns at the Triana Bridge. It was, however, in Madrid, where I finished "A Fali".

I would spend my next five years in Madrid where I composed the five remaining pieces that make up this first book and immersed myself in different facets of the world of flamenco guitar such as voice and dance accompaniment and solo playing. While I continued with Rafael's teachings, I started working with great artists who served as the inspiration for the composition of the other works.

Madrid's autumn is reflected in my *taranta*, "*Calle de la Memoria*" (Street of Memories), composed back in 2012 while I wa on an international tour with renowned *bailaores* and *cantaores*. At that time, I also learned about the solitude of practicing the guitar, the "*Cárcel de Oro*" (Prison of Gold) as maestro Manolo Sanlúcar described it. That is why I chose this title for th *solea*. The love and passions that surround the world of art in general, and music in particular— were the inspiration for my *guajira*, "*La Calzada de la Reina*" (The Queen's Dancing Shoes). It was composed in 2014 in Madrid, during a period when I was touring extensively with some of the top flamenco dancers. I was asked to write a guajira for the dancer, María Juncal, so I came up with this piece, which honors the beauty of flamenco dancing and all of the great dancers that have introduced flamenco culture to the world.

Almonaster la Real is the name of an ancient village in the province of Huelva in southwest Spain. I spent a lot of time there in 2010, composing and studying with Rafael Riqueni, so the town has a lot of meaning for me. The title, "Por Almonaster" means "In" or "At Almonaster", honoring the town and its citizens and remembering the times I enjoyed there.

The *buleria*, "*Generaciones*" (Generations) is a tribute to the new generation that is fighting to gain a foothold in the world o flamenco guitar, a new modern touch that blends the influences of the great masters. This piece is a synthesis of everything I experienced during my formative years, expressed through the guitar.

I hope you enjoy playing these pieces!

"The soul of a child is always innocent, always flying towards the unknown in search of an impossible dream. Navigating between illusions, always with a wide smile and an open heart, it abandons the intellect and never pretends, but overflows with intelligence and freedom, a sober madness that defies established norms. I hope this work inspires you and awakens the child in you."

Yago Santos

Contents

About the Audio and Video Recordings

stute listeners will notice that three cuts on the *Alma de Niño* album feature an improvised, econd guitar accompaniment part: “La Calzada de la Reina”, “Por Almonaster” and Generaciones”. Nonetheless, these pieces can be played successfully as flamenco guitar solos.

About the Author

ago Santos is a *summa cum laude* graduate of The Berklee College of Music in Boston, the inner of the first “Paco de Lucia Prize” at the Seville International Guitar Competition, and e recipient of a 2022 Fulbright Scholarship. He holds a PhD in Music and its Science and echnology from the Polytechnic University of Madrid and the Queen Sofía School of Music.

ago collaborated with film composers Hans Zimmer and Lorne Balfe on the EMI-nominated ational Geographic series, “Genius: Picasso” and works as a composer for companies such niversal, Sony ATV and BMG among others.

s part of a new generation of guitarists gaining a foothold in the flamenco world, Yago Santos a disciple of maestro Rafael Riqueni. He has toured internationally as a soloist and shared the age with such flamenco luminaries as José Merce, Manuel Molina, El Pele, José el de la Tomasa, layte Martín, and his former teacher and mentor—Rafael Riqueni.

lma de Niño was Santos’ first CD recording, followed by *Homage to Claude Debussy*.

A mi maestro, Rafael Riqueni

A FALI - PRELUDE

Solea por Buleria

Capo II

② → **A**
⑥ → **D**

YAGO SANTOS
(Sevilla, 2019)

Tempo rubato

a tempo
più cresc.
fp tranquilo
f rápido
p ... simile
dim.
mf

rit.
10
a m i m a m
pp sempre
TAB

A mi maestro, Rafael Riqueni

A FALI

Solea por Buleria

Capo II
② → **A**
⑥ → **D**

YAGO SANTOS
(Sevilla, 2019)

Allegro ♩=147

ff
mp subito

19
21
p i m a m i
23
25
p … sigue
mf espress.
27

p … sigue
f espress.
p … sigue

p ... sigue
TAB

49
a m i p i p p i
p p p p p p … sigue
51
p p i p p
p … sigue
53
i i p … sigue i
55
i p … sigue
p i p i p i p i p … sigue
57
i i p … sigue i
p e i p e i p e i p e i p m
TAB

p … sigue

p … sigue

89
91
93
p … sigue
95
97
p …
TAB

p ...... simile

109
p i m a
111
p i m a m p
113
p
p i m p
m
115
p i p i p ... sigue
117
p i p ... sigue
i
p ... sigue
p
legato

119
121
123
125
127

139
141
p … sigue
143
p … sigue
145
147

149
151
p .... simile
rasg. sigue
153
accel.
155
157
TAB

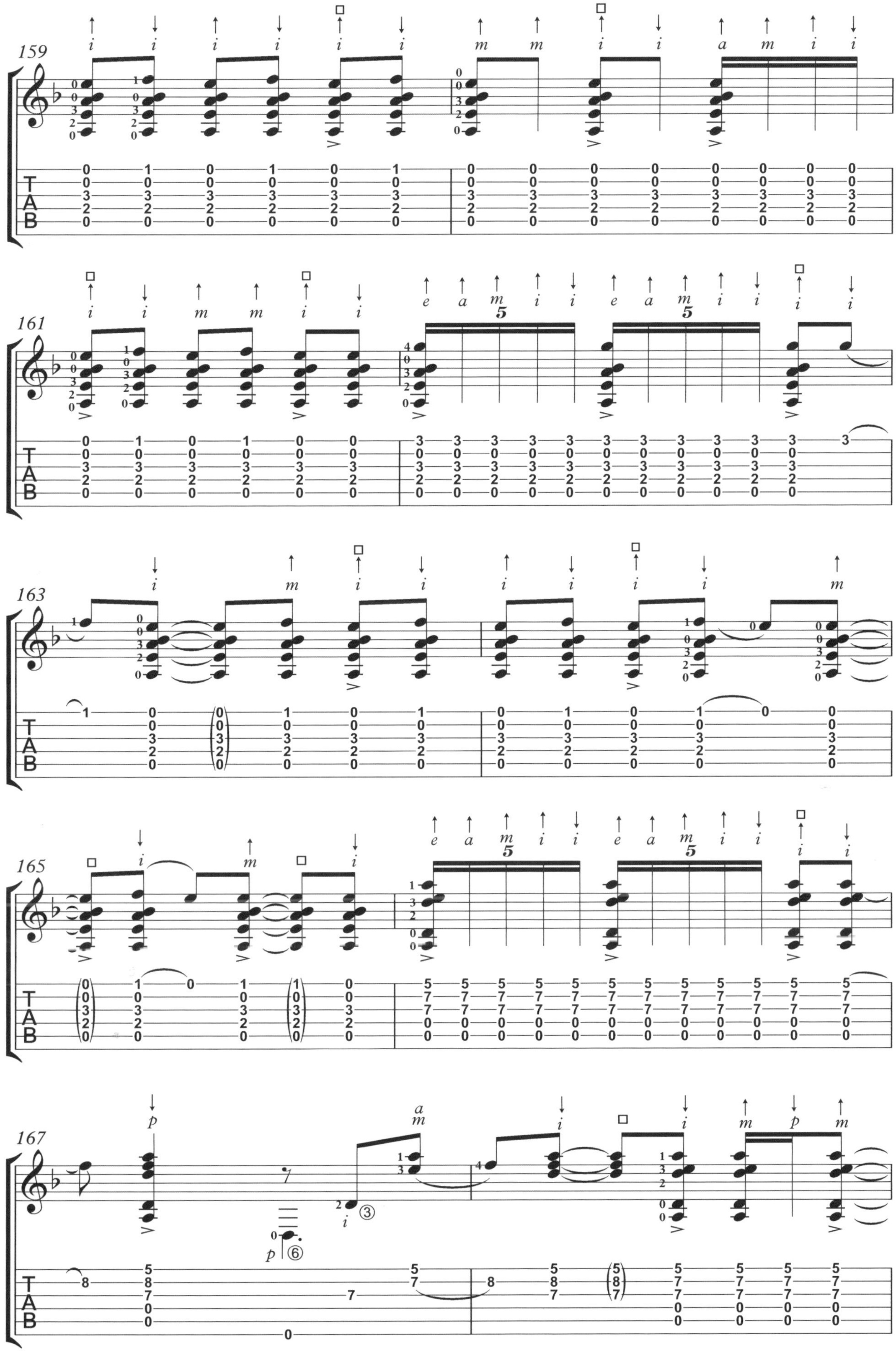
159
161
163
165
167
T
A
B

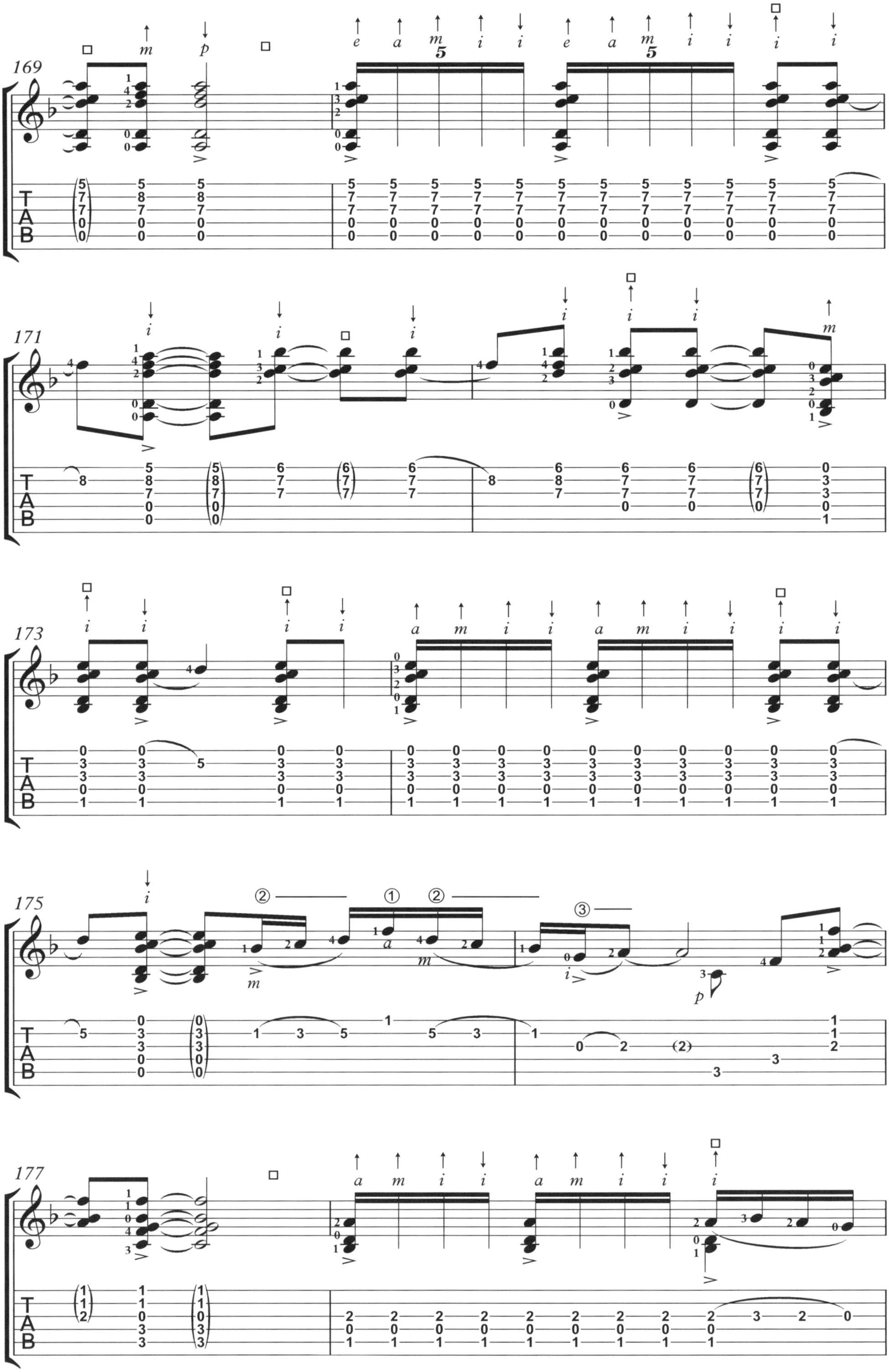
169
171
173
175
177

179
p … sigue
181
p … sigue
183
185
p … sigue
m i m i m i m … sigue
rápido
187

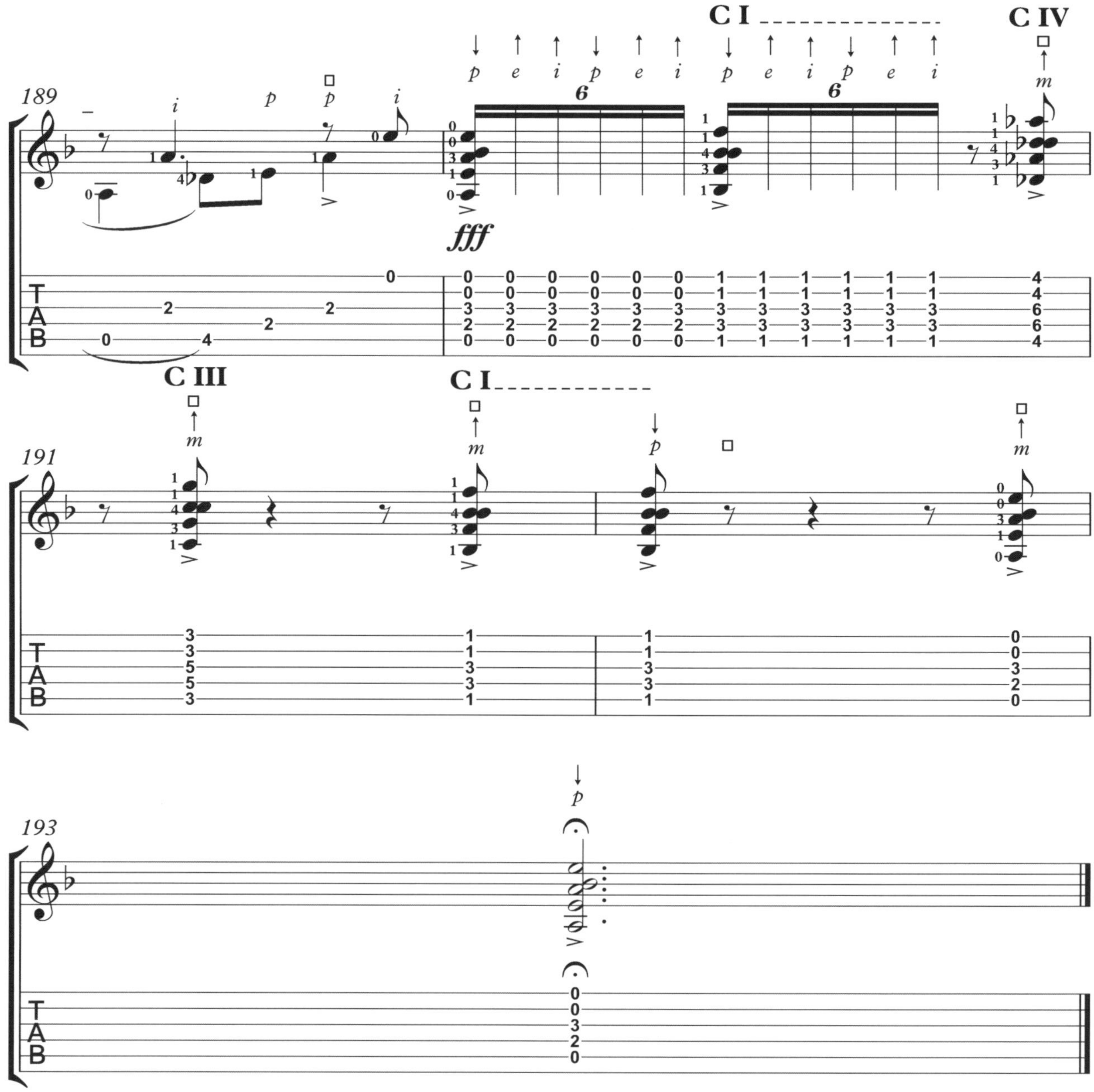
C I
C IV
189
6
fff
T
A
B
C III
C I
191
193

CALLE DE LA MEMORIA

Taranta

YAGO SANTOS
(Sevilla, 2019)

Capo I

ad libitum

C II
cresc.
mf
mp
meno
pesante
arpegg. lento
f
molto dim.
legato
simile

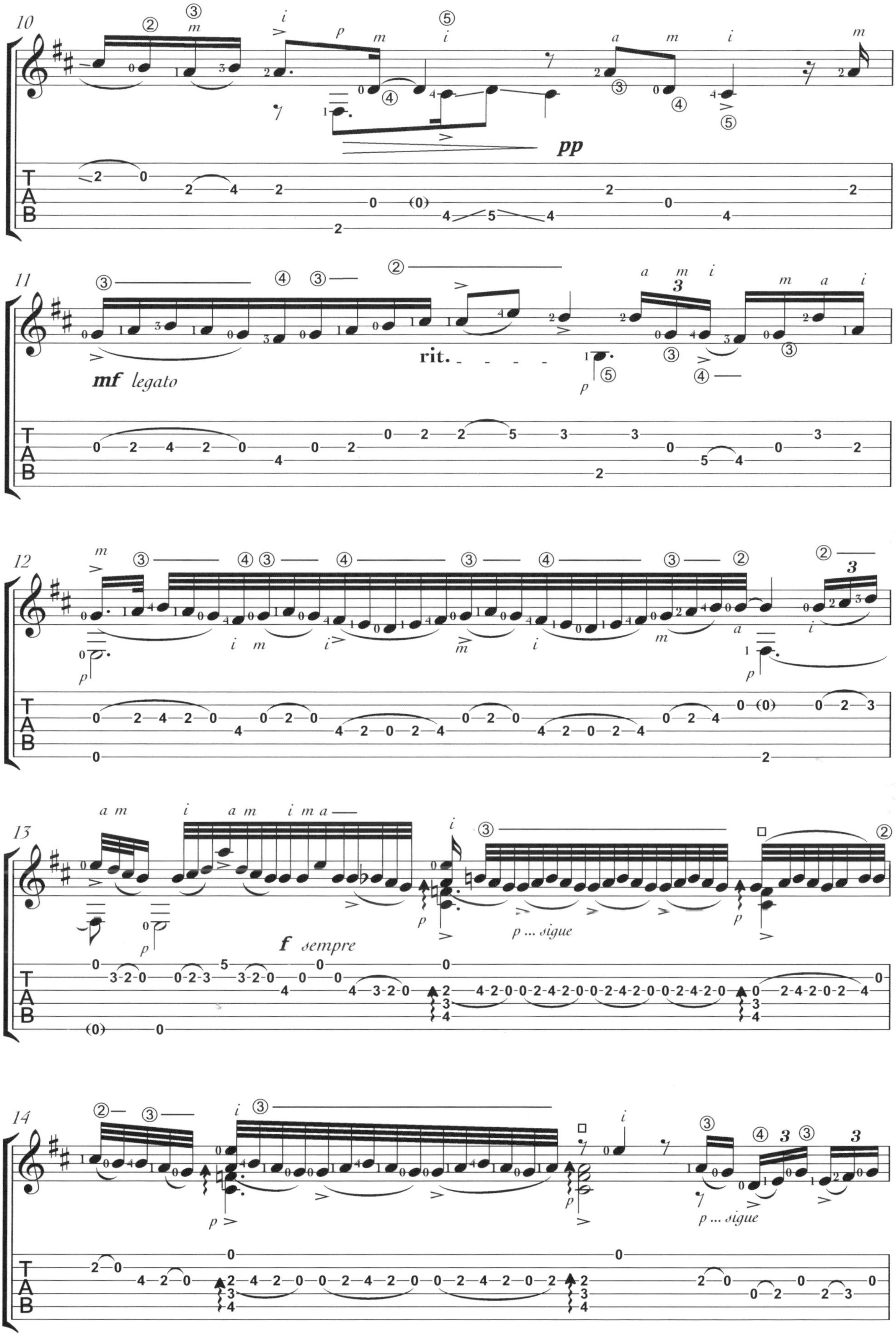
10
pp
11
mf legato
rit.
12
13
f sempre
p ... sigue
14
p ... sigue

15
16
17
dim.
18
m a p p i m a i p p p i m a
mp
mf
legato
p
fp
p
mp legato
19
p
sfz
p
dolce

C II
i m ... sigue
mf
ff
mf
dim.
C VII
p i m a m i ... simile

accel.
p p i m a m i a m i a m i m...
ff
p i m a m i a m i a m i m...
pp
C VII
i m i... simile
mp
C V
i m i... simile

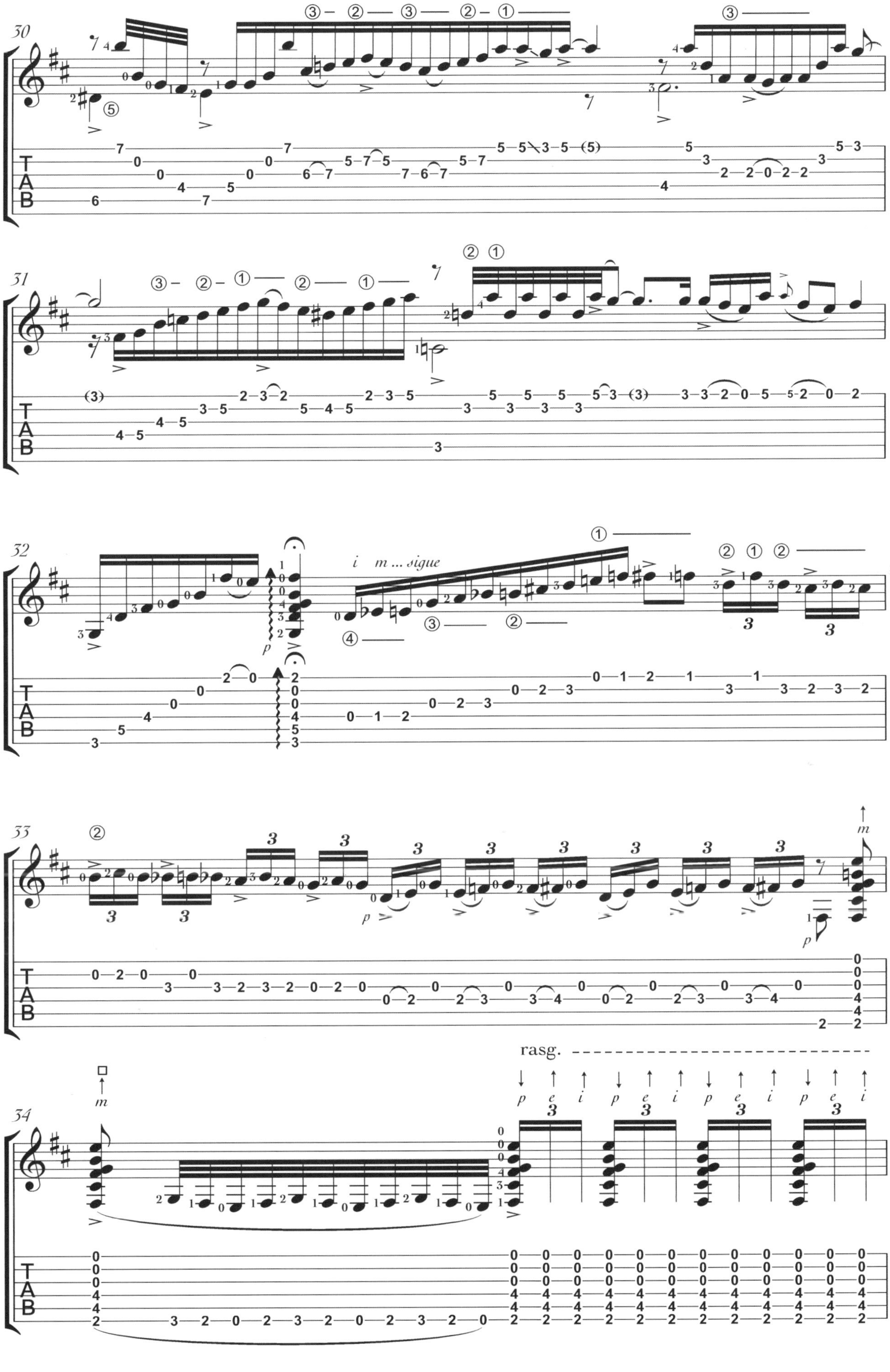
i m ... sigue
rasg.

p ... sigue
p ... sigue

poco rall.
mp espress.
mf
dim.
pp
f

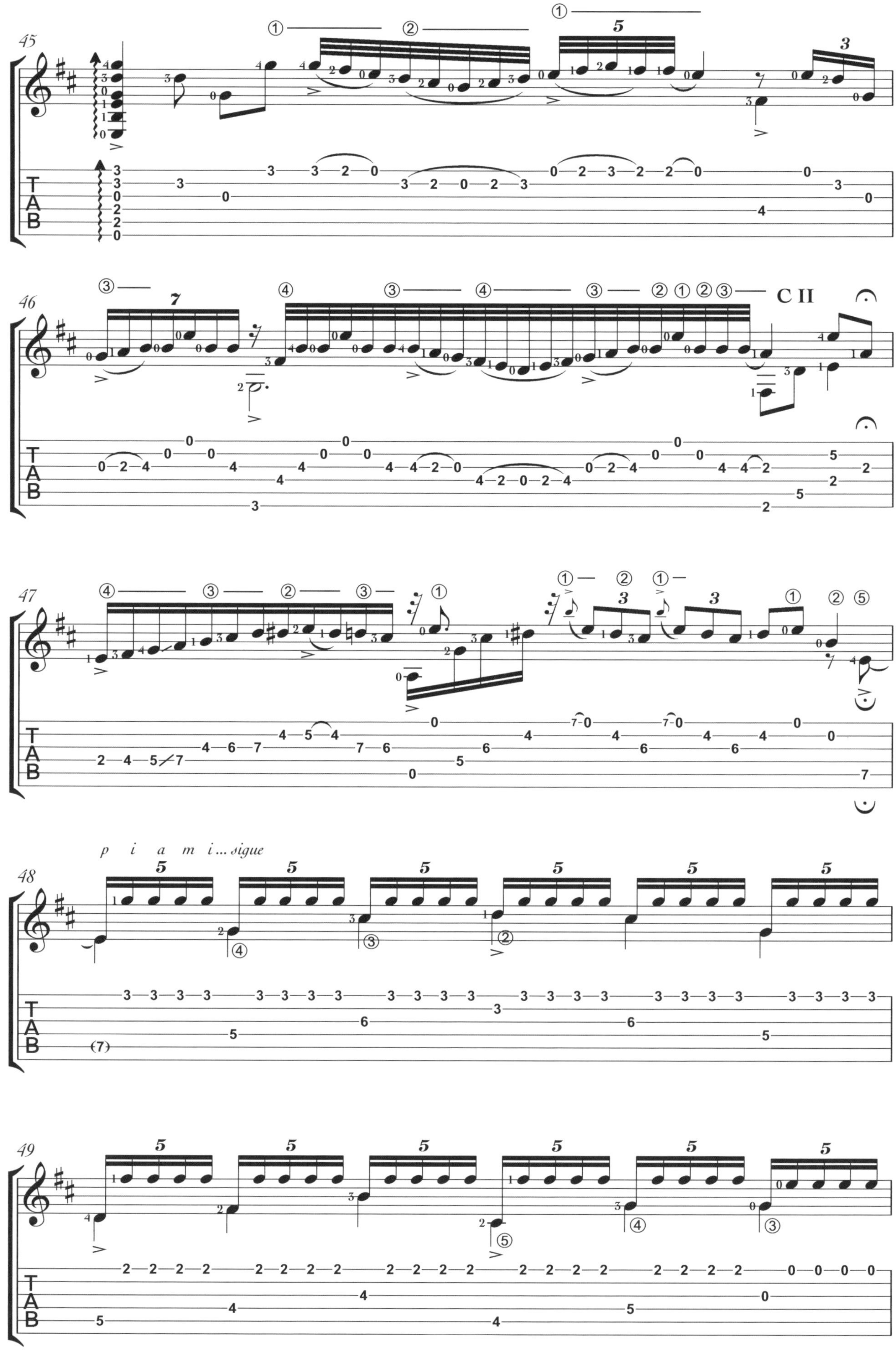
C II
p i a m i... sigue

p i a m i ... sigue

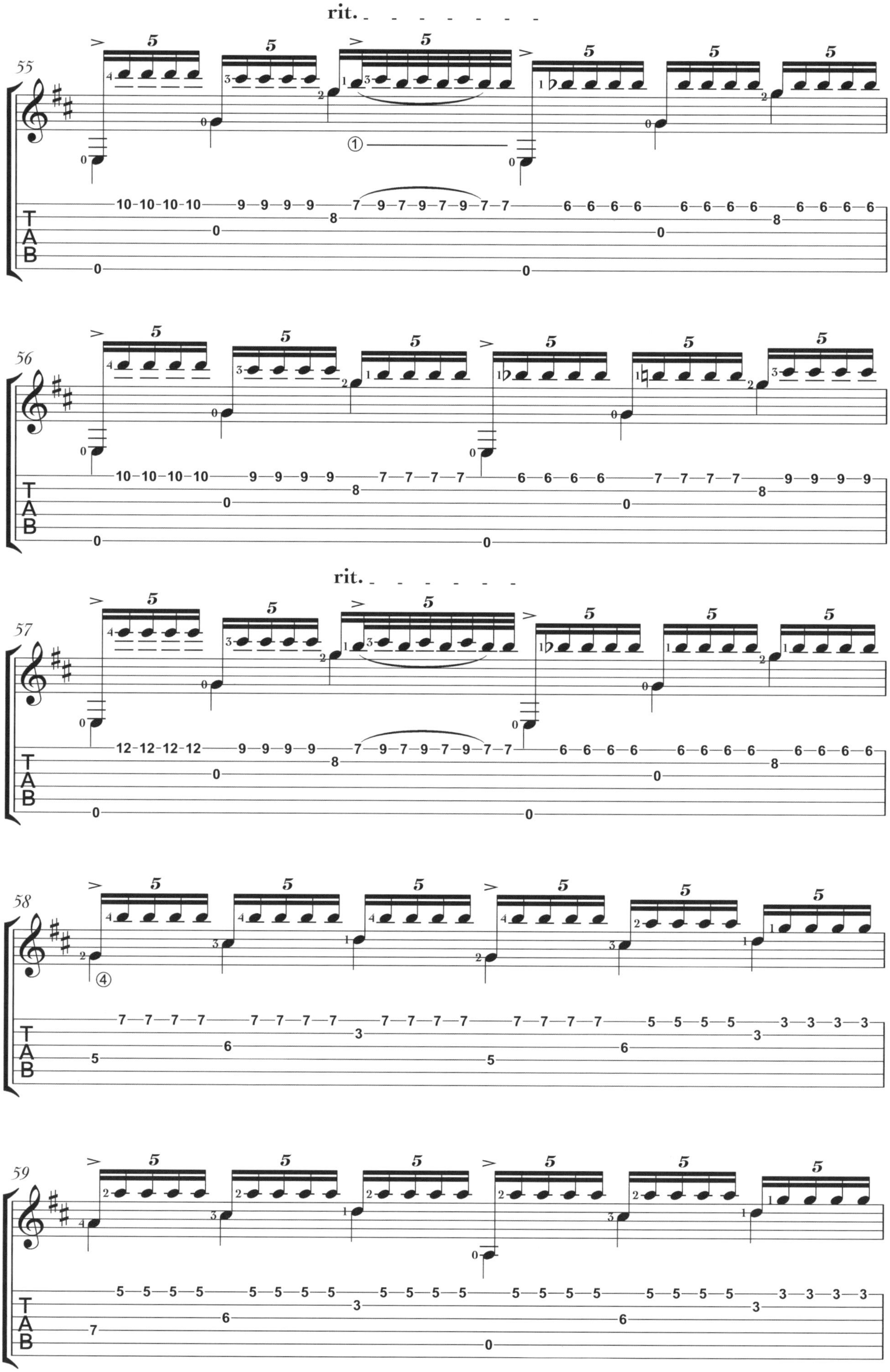
rit.
55
rit.
57
58
59

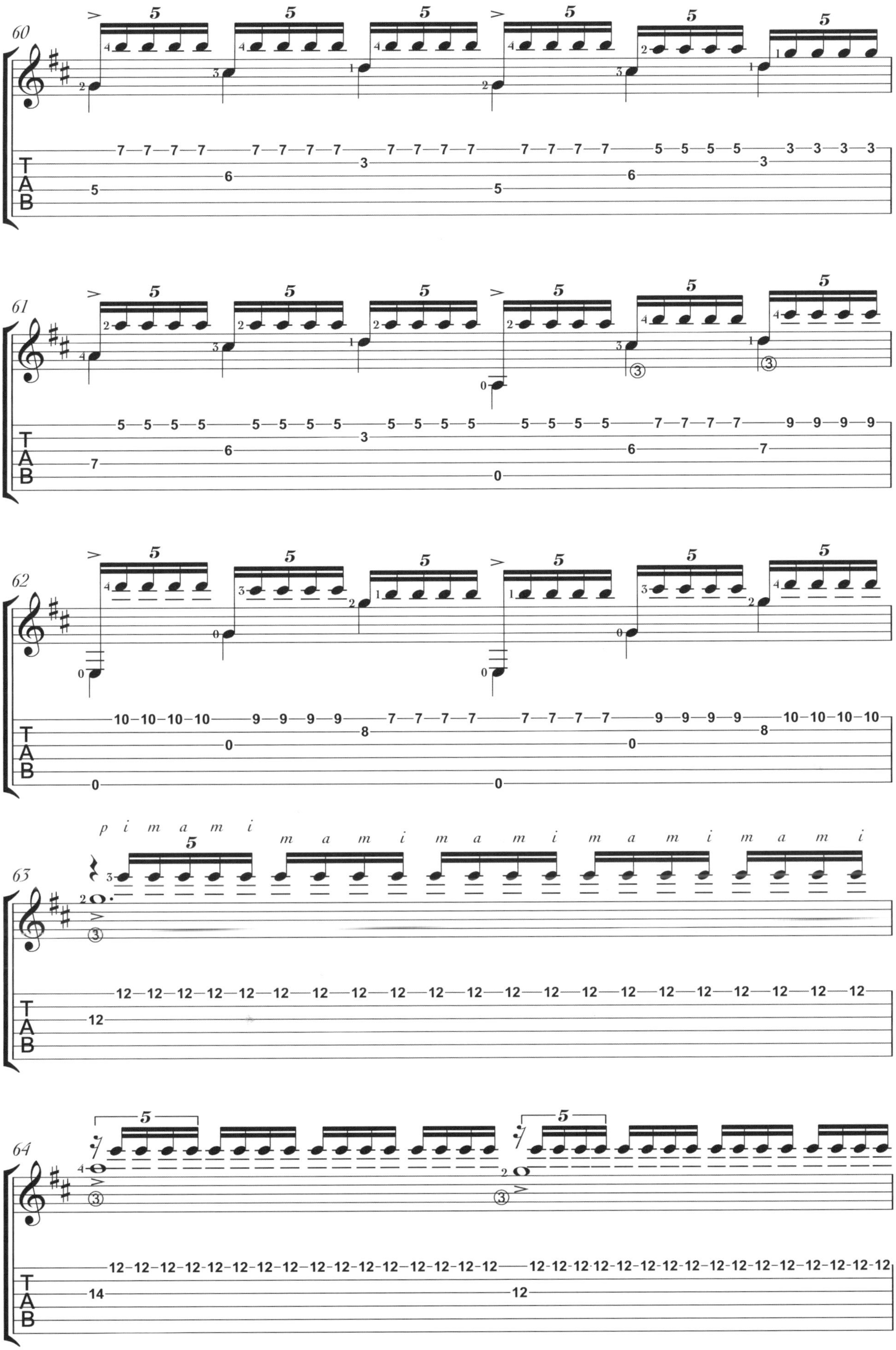
60
61
62
63
p i m a m i
m a m i m a m i m a m i m a m i
64
TAB

65
66
67
68
C III
69

mf legato
ad libitum
f sempre
ff

LA CALZADA DE LA REINA

Guajira

Capo I

Moderato q= 120

YAGO SANTOS
(Sevilla, 2019)

meno
mf espress.
più dim.
C II
sfz
poco crec.

19
f leggiero
21
marcato
23
f
legato
25
meno
27
dolce
cresc.

molto dim.
mf cantabile
C II
C V
C IV
C II

39
41
m i m i ... sigue
43
poco cresc.
45
f
47
dim.

mp espress.
poco cresc.
mf
meno
poco meno
mf

f vibrante
mp
f vibrante
mp
C IV
tranquilo

C II
molto cresc.
ff
p ... sigue

p ... sigue
legato
meno
cresc.
mp cantabile

89
91
mf
93
f sempre
dolce
95
mp espress.
97
f

99
101
mf
103
dim.
105
107

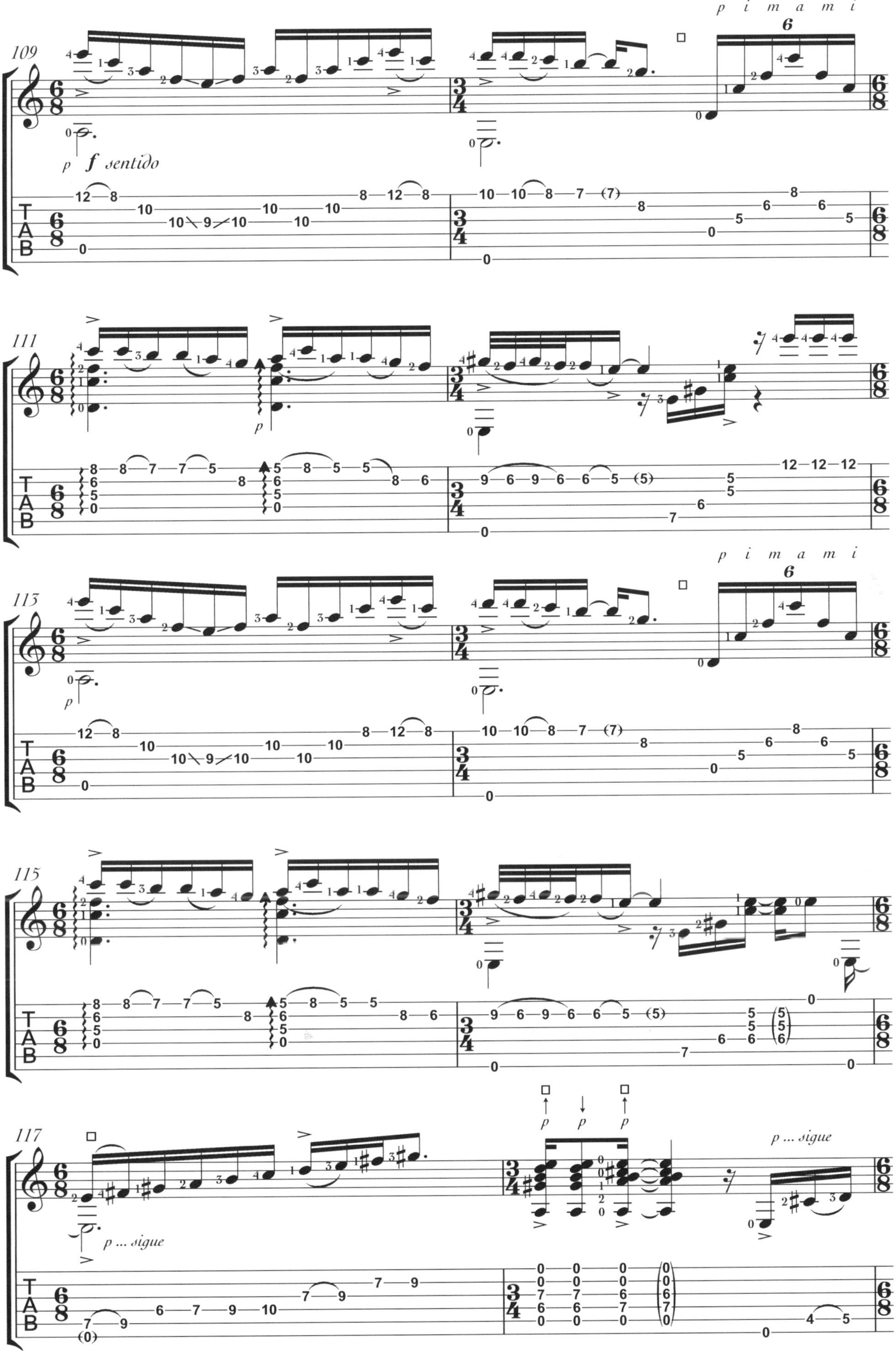
109
p f sentido
p i m a m i
6
111
113
p i m a m i
6
115
117
p ... sigue
p ... sigue

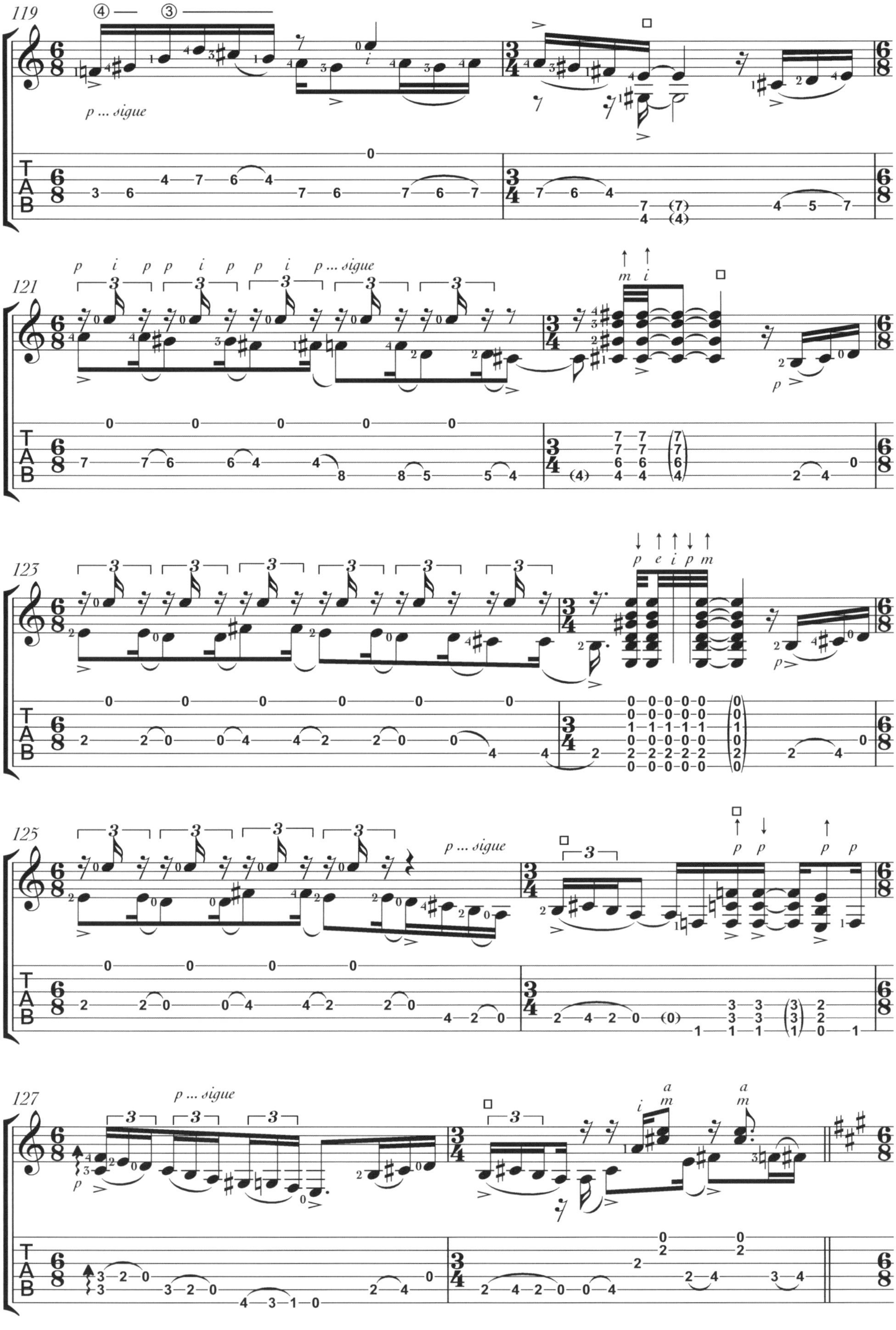
119
p ... sigue
121
p i p p i p p i p ... sigue
m i
123
p e i p m
125
p ... sigue
p p p p
127
p ... sigue
i a m a m

129
cresc.
131
cresc.
f
133
135
137
mp dolce
cresc poco a poco

mf
C II
C II
dim.
cresc.
f sempre

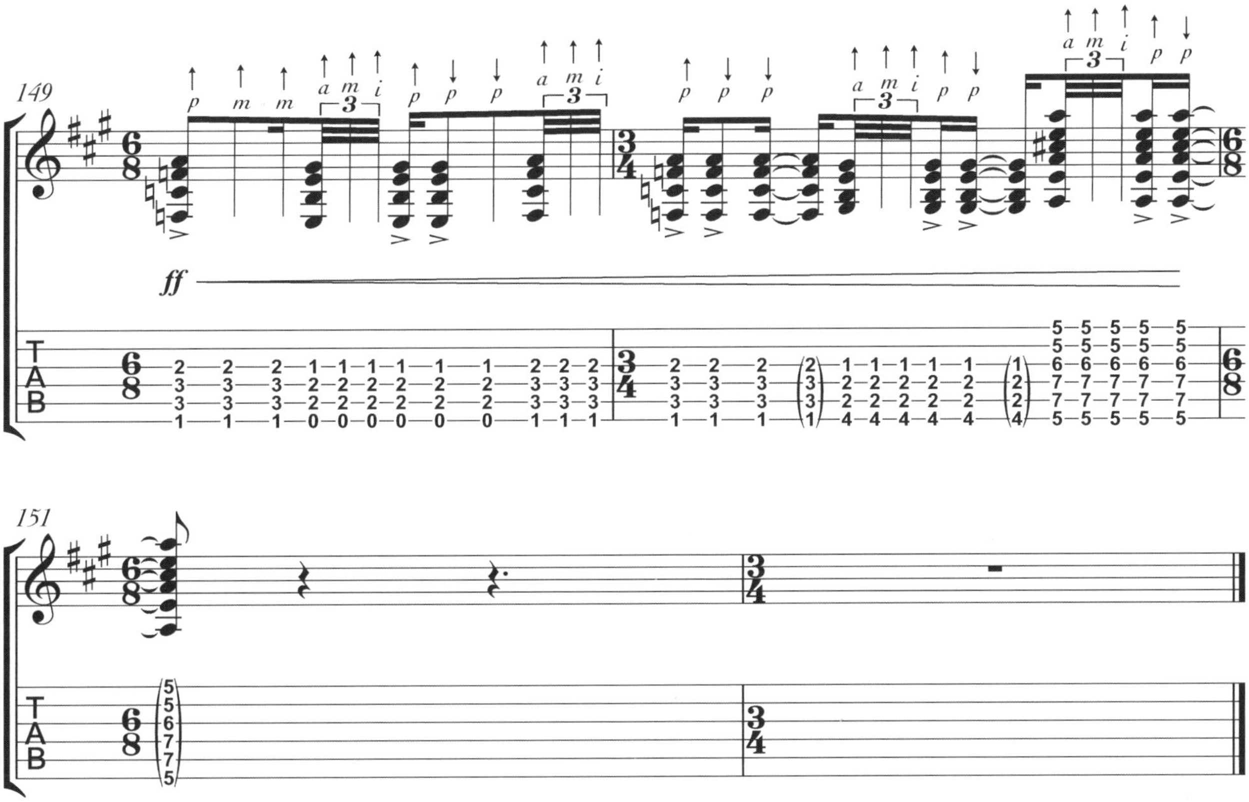
149
p m m a m i
p p p a m i
p p p a m i p p
a m i p p
ff
T
A
B
151

CÁRCEL DE ORO

Solea

YAGO SANTOS
(Sevilla, 2019)

Capo I

Andante ♩= 10(

a tempo
p ... sigue
legato
legato
p ... sigue

p ... sigue
ff leggiero

rasg.
f sempre

p ... sigue
mp
p ...

50
p ... sigue
mf
52
p i m a m i
f
54
p ... sigue
mf
56
meno
58
i m i m ... sigue
mf
f
dim.
i m a m i a m i

60
p i m a m i
62
i m i m...
mf
f
∂im.
64
66
p .... sigue
68

p ... sigue
ff

90
p i a m i p i a m i ... sigue
mp molto espress.
92
mf
94
dim.
96
98
dolce

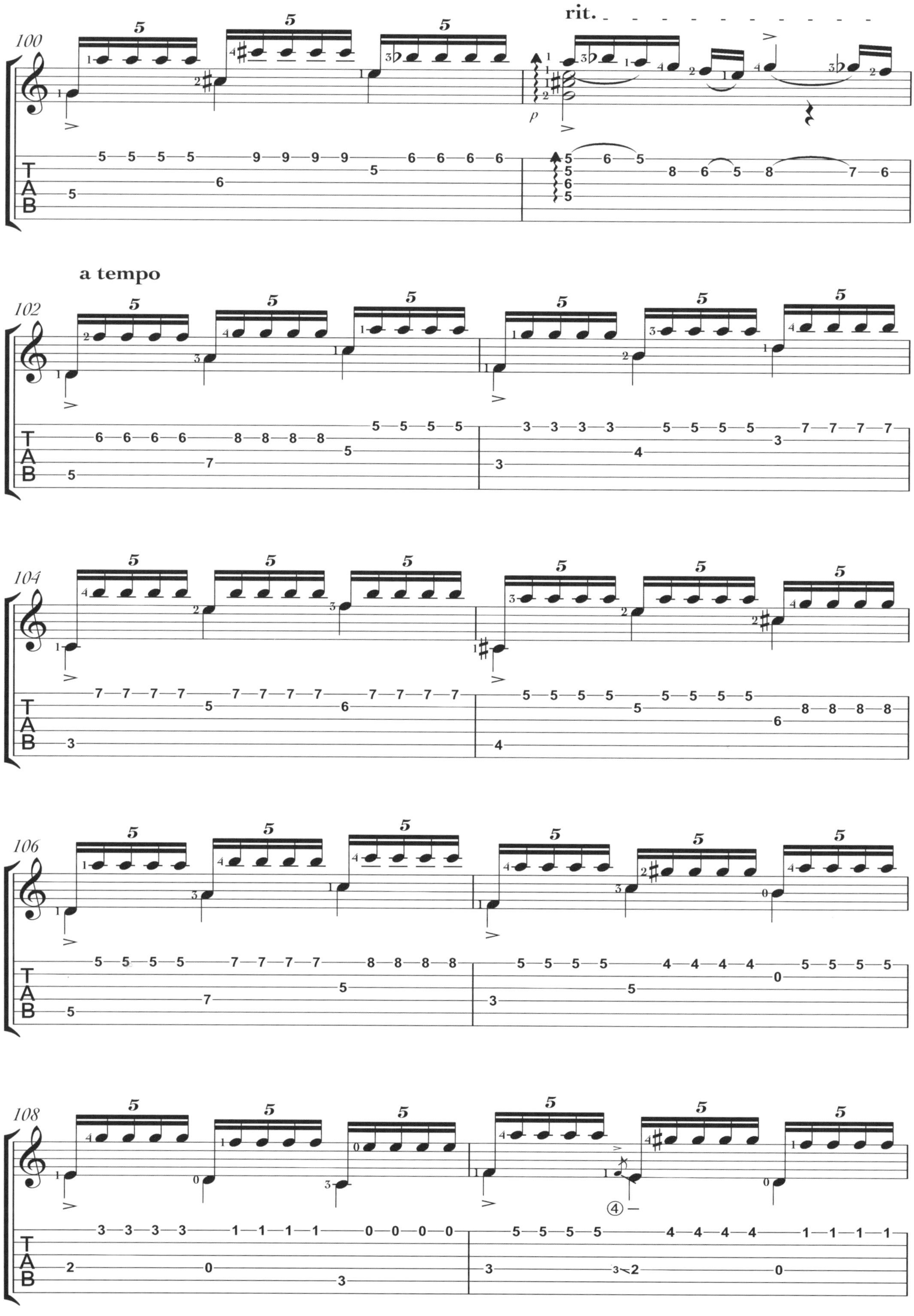
rit.
a tempo

110
112
114
116
118

120
122
p i m a m p
m p i m p...
124
126
128

p ... sigue

140
p i p i
p i m a m i p i m a m i
a m i a m i m i m
142
p i a m i ... sigue
144
146
148

150
152
154
156
158
TAB

160
162
164
accel.
presto
166
168

170
172
174
cresc.
176
178
cresc.
f

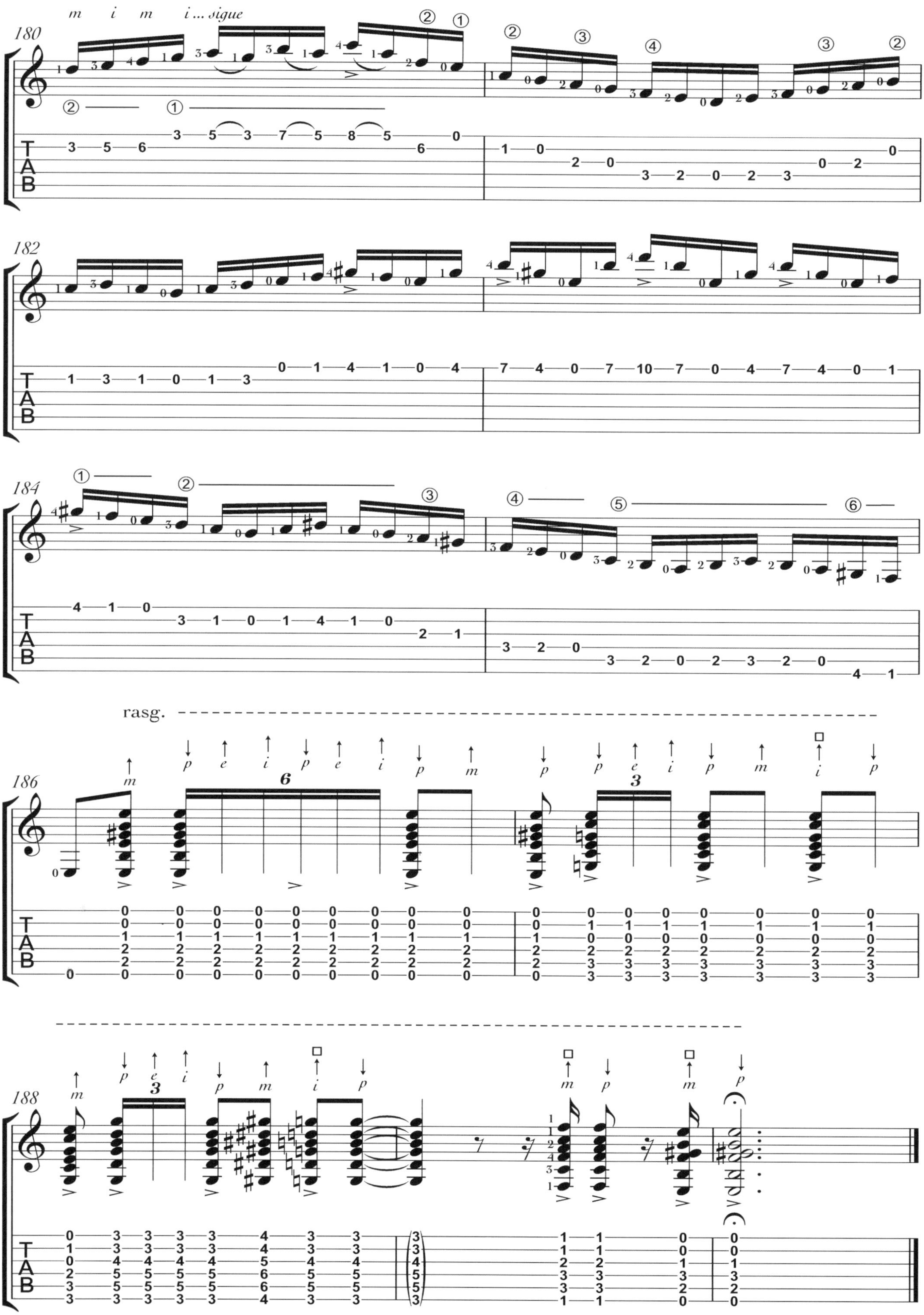
180
m i m i ... sigue
182
184
rasg.
186
188
p e i p e i p m
p p e i p m i p
m p e i p m i p
m p m p

POR ALMONASTER - INTERLUDE

Fandangos de Huelva

YAGO SANTOS
(Sevilla, 2019)

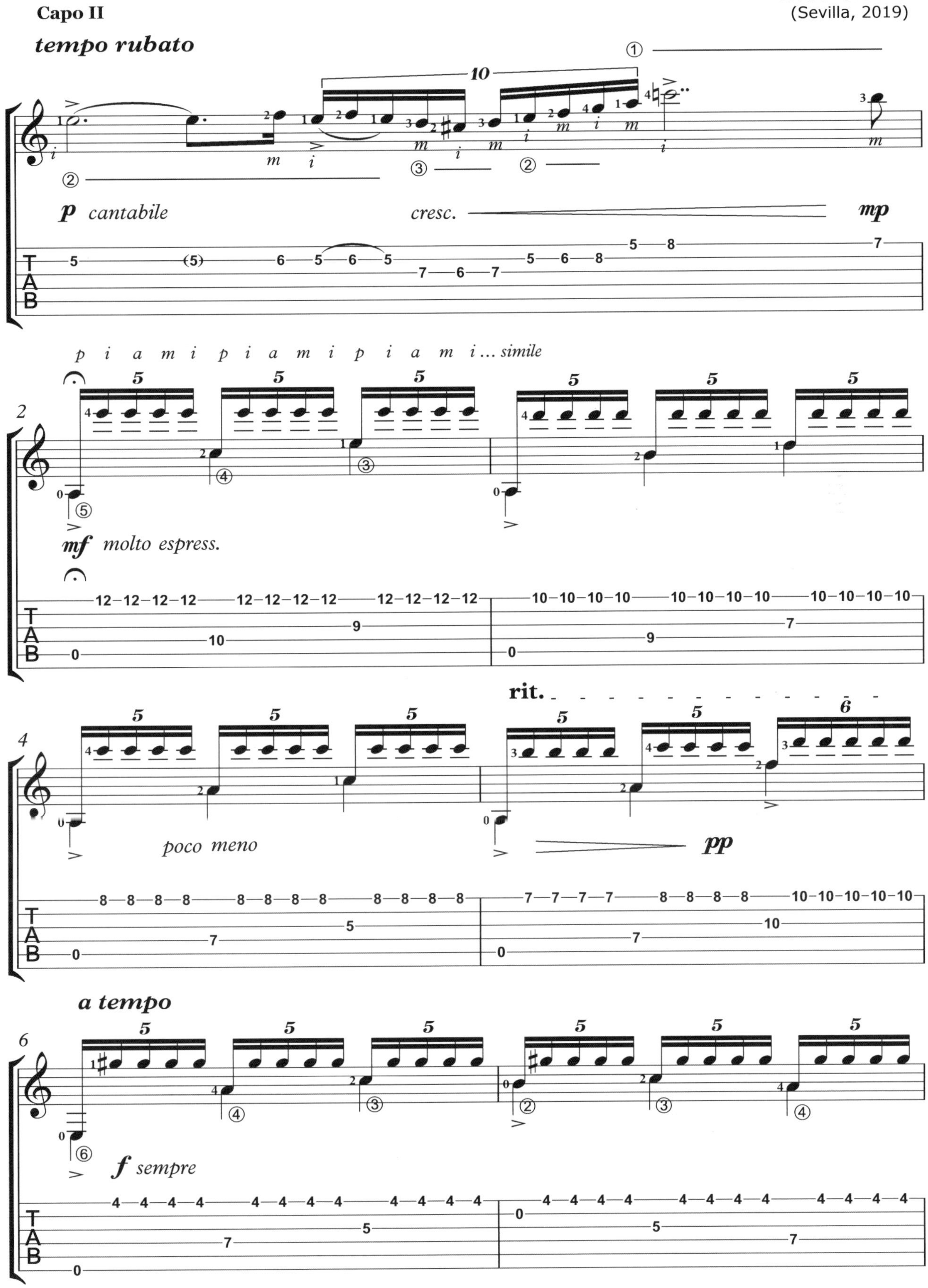

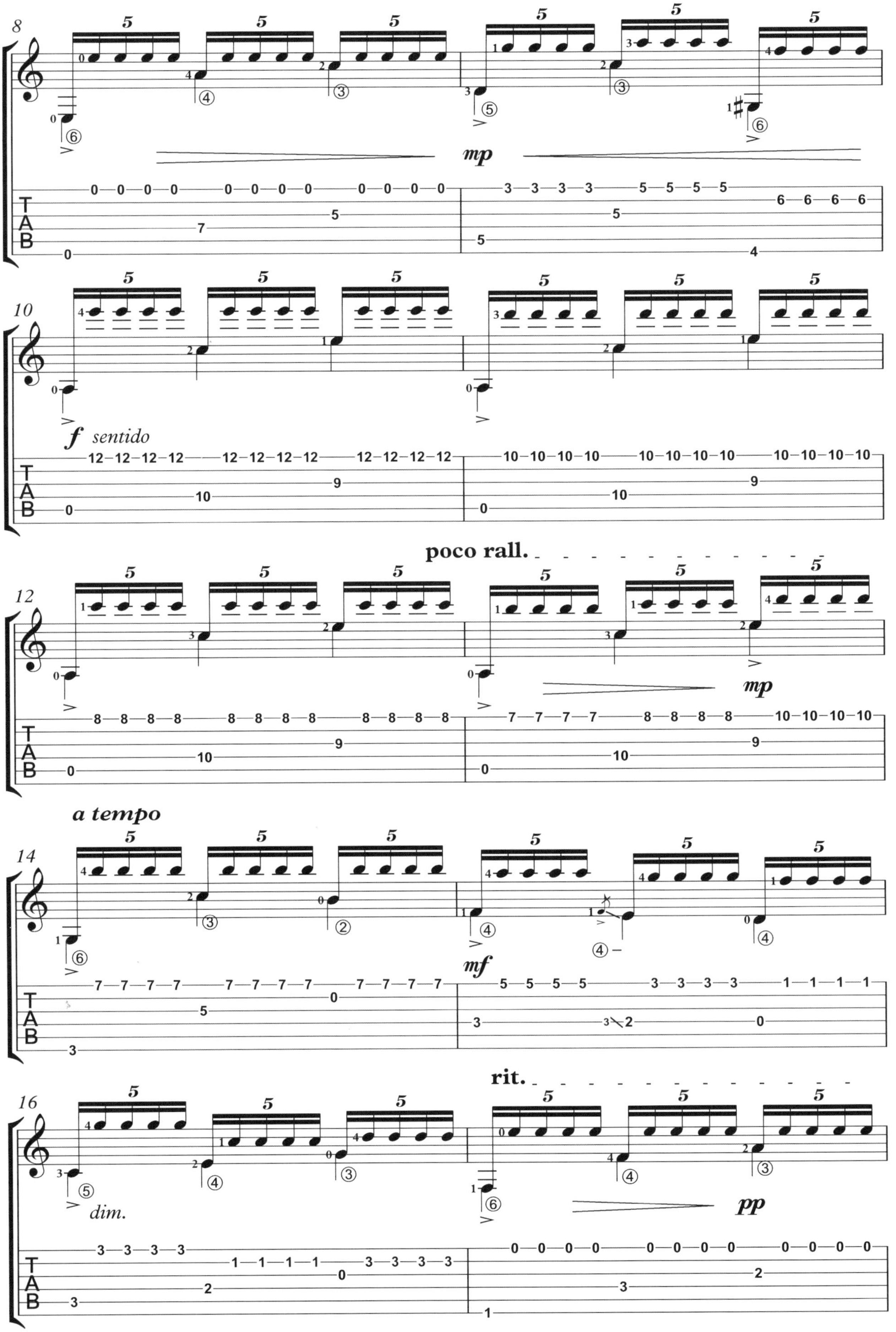
mp
f sentido
poco rall.
mp
a tempo
mf
rit.
dim.
pp

a tempo
dolce sostenuto
brillante
ad libitum
rápido
poco rall.
molto dim

28
p
molto dim
30
pp
32
TAB

POR ALMONASTER

Fandangos de Huelva

Capo II

Tempo ♩.=140

YAGO SANTOS
(Sevilla, 2019)

poco cresc.
legato

19
cresc.
f
21
mf dolcemente.
23
25
27
i m ...simile
f rápido

i m i … simile
meno
mf

a m i p i m i ... sigue
mp espress.
p a m i p i m i ... simile

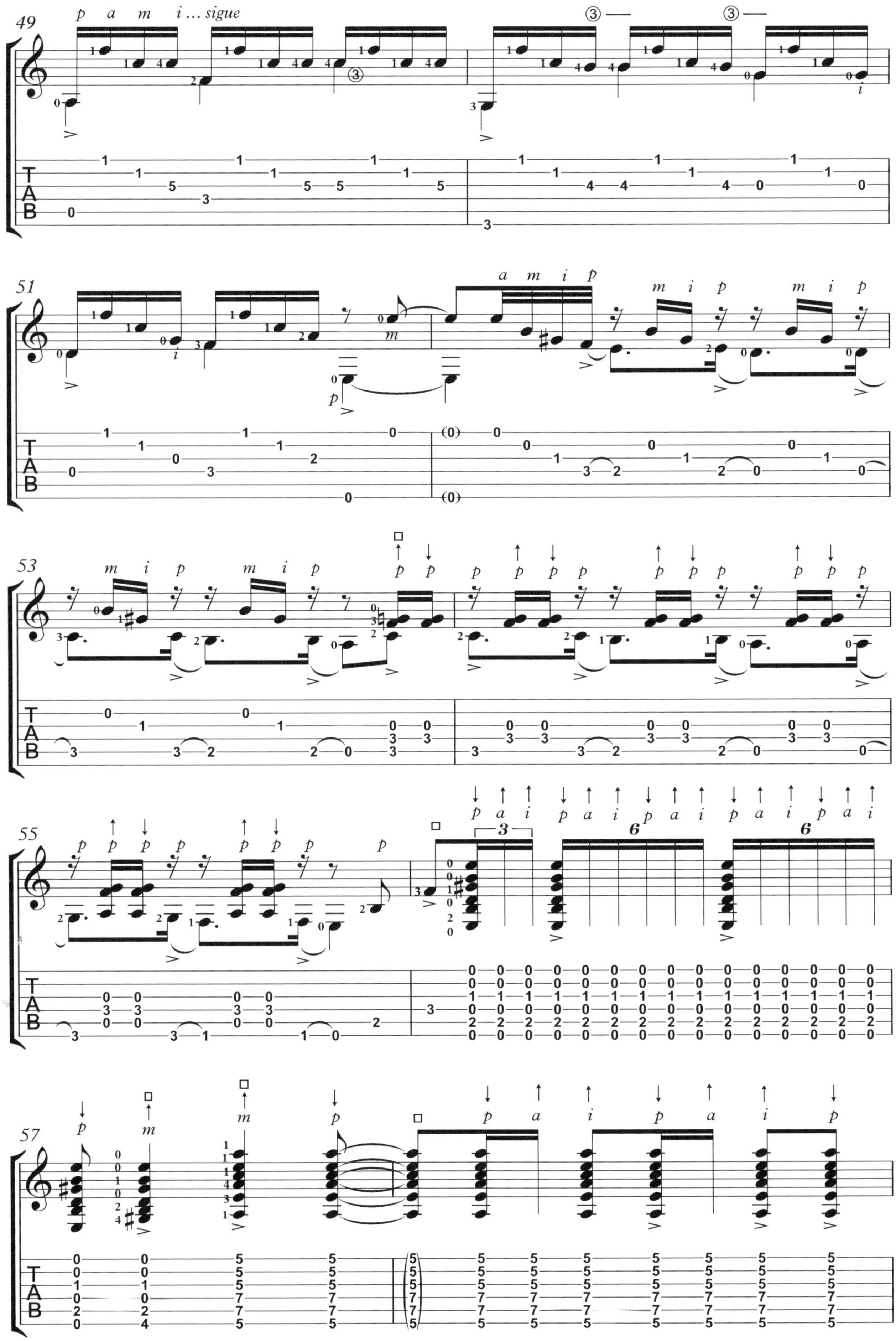
p a m i … sigue

59
61
63
65
67

69
71
p … sigue
73
75
77

p ... sigue
mf
f
meno
mp

p … sigue
p … sigue

p … sigue

p .... sigue

mp espress.

139
141
143
145
147
p … simile

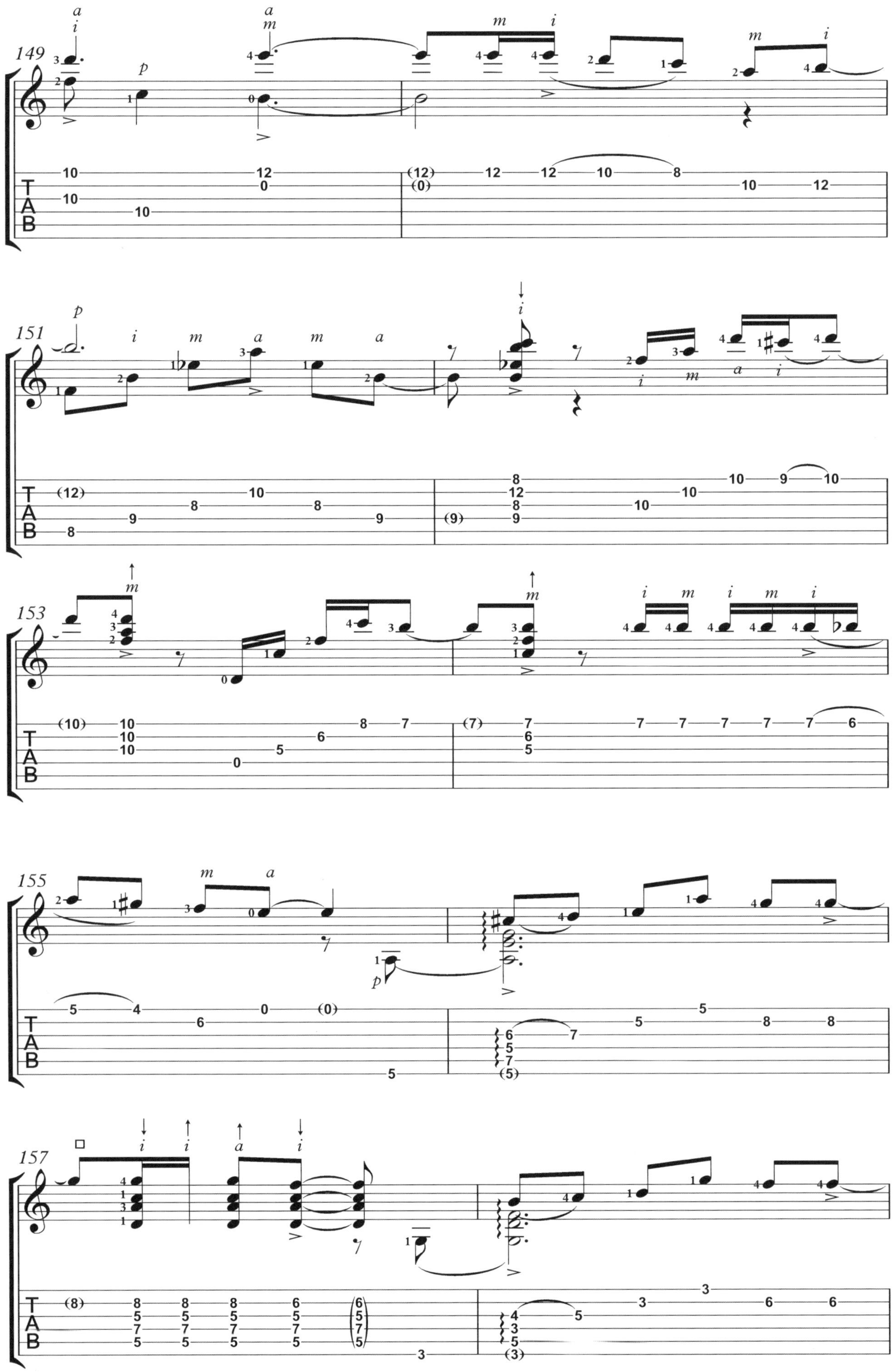

159
i i a i
TAB
161
i i a i
163
a m i p
leggiero
p m i p m i p m
165
p a m i p a m i p m
p a m i p a m i p m
167
p a m i p a m i p a m i
p a m i a m i a m i

169
171
173
175
177
TAB

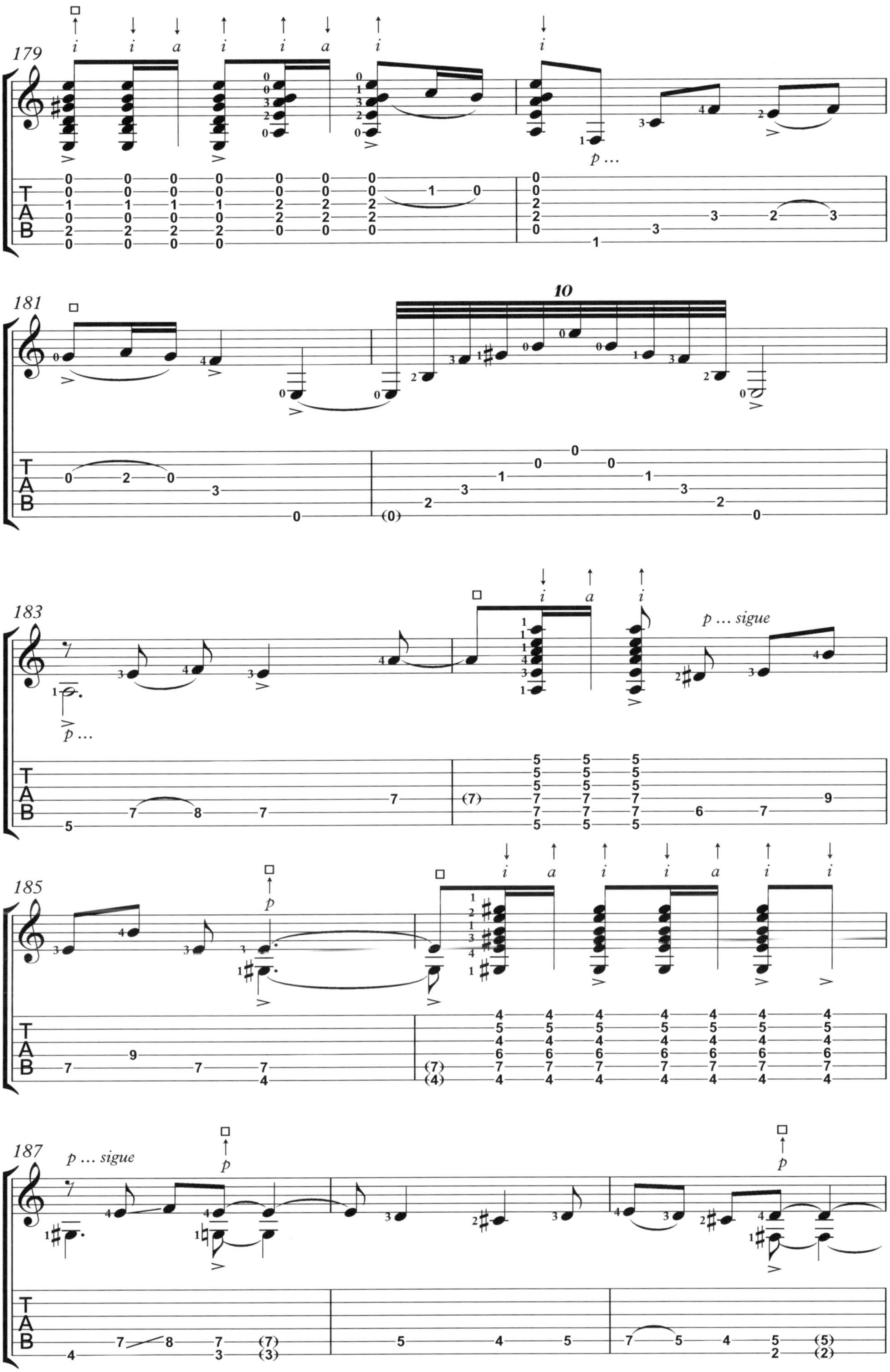
179
p …
181
10
183
p …
p … sigue
185
187
p … sigue

190
192
p … sigue
194
196
198
TAB

200
203
p … sigue
205
207
p …….. sigue
209

211
p … sigue
213
215
p … simile
217
219
p … simile

221
223
225
227
229
TAB

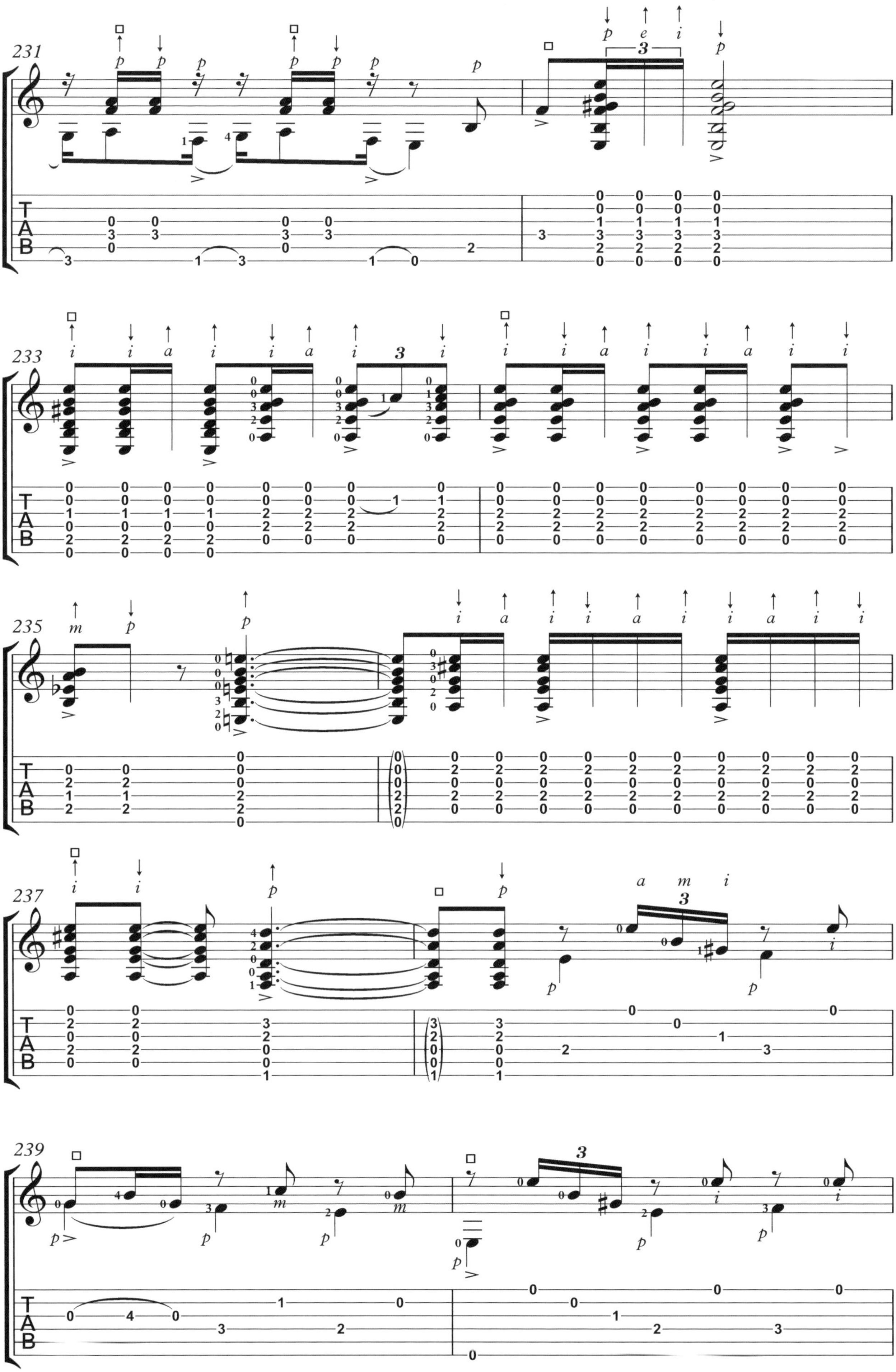
231
233
235
237
239

241
243
245
247
249

251
253
255
257
259
C V
C III
p mute
TAB

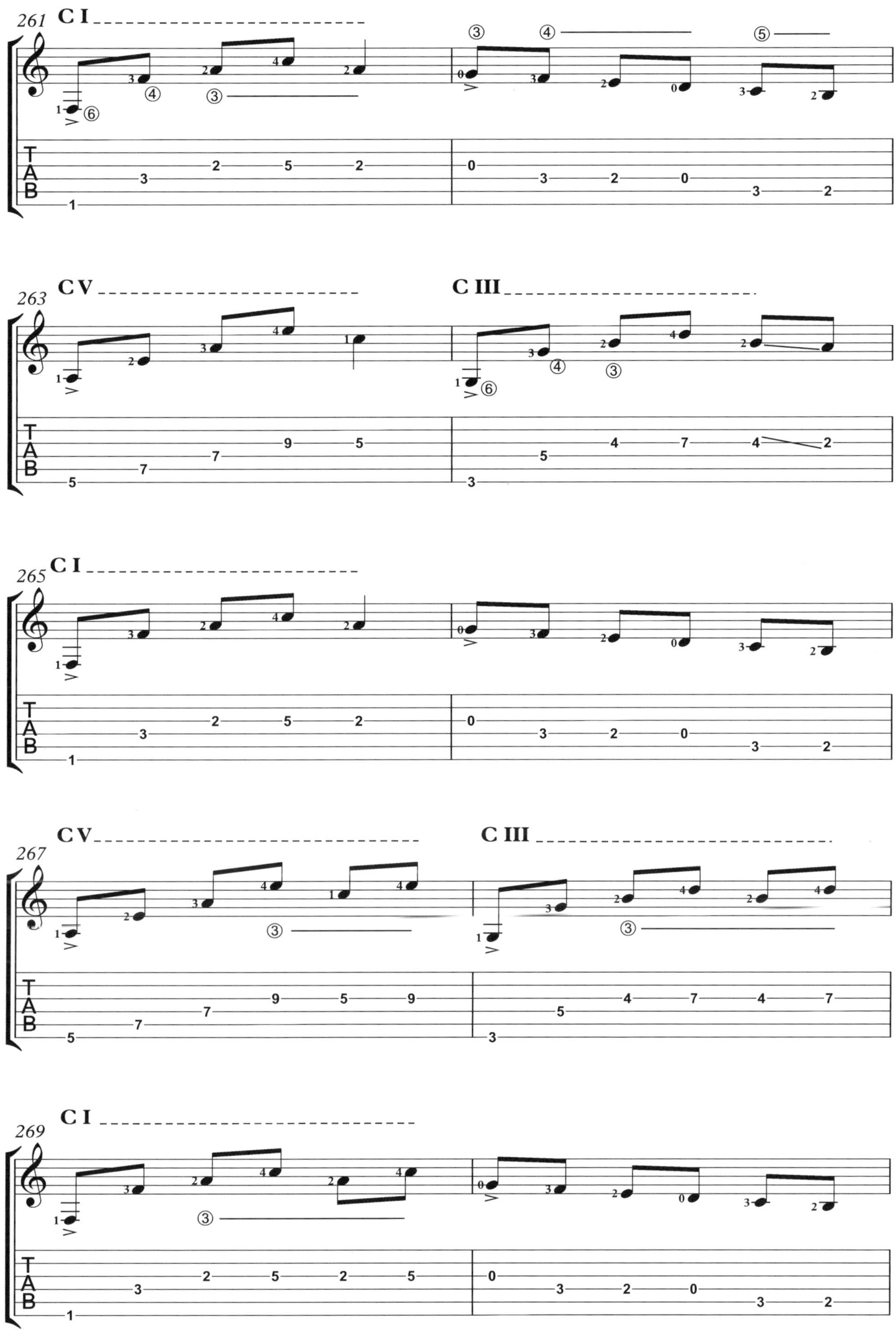
261
C I
263
C V
C III
265
C I
267
C V
C III
269
C I

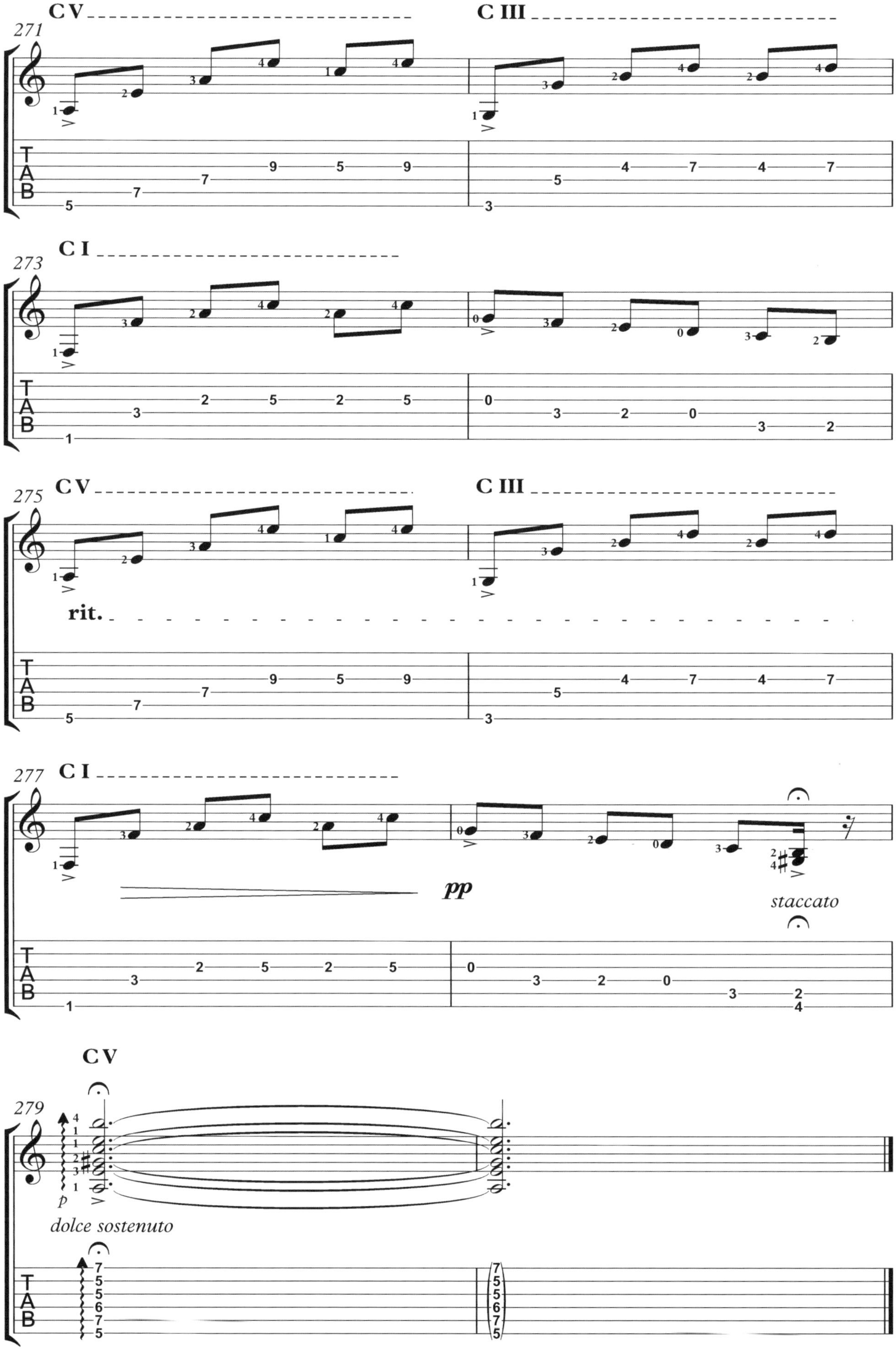
271
C V
C III
273
C I
275
C V
C III
rit.
277
C I
pp
staccato
C V
279
p
dolce sostenuto
TAB

GENERACIONES

Buleria

YAGO SANTOS
(Sevilla, 2019)

Capo III

Vivo ♩= 120

C III
C V
p … sigue
p … sigue

C III

p .... simile
p .... simile

40
42
p .... simile
44
p .... simile
46
48
p … sigue
TAB

50
52
54
56
58
CV
TAB

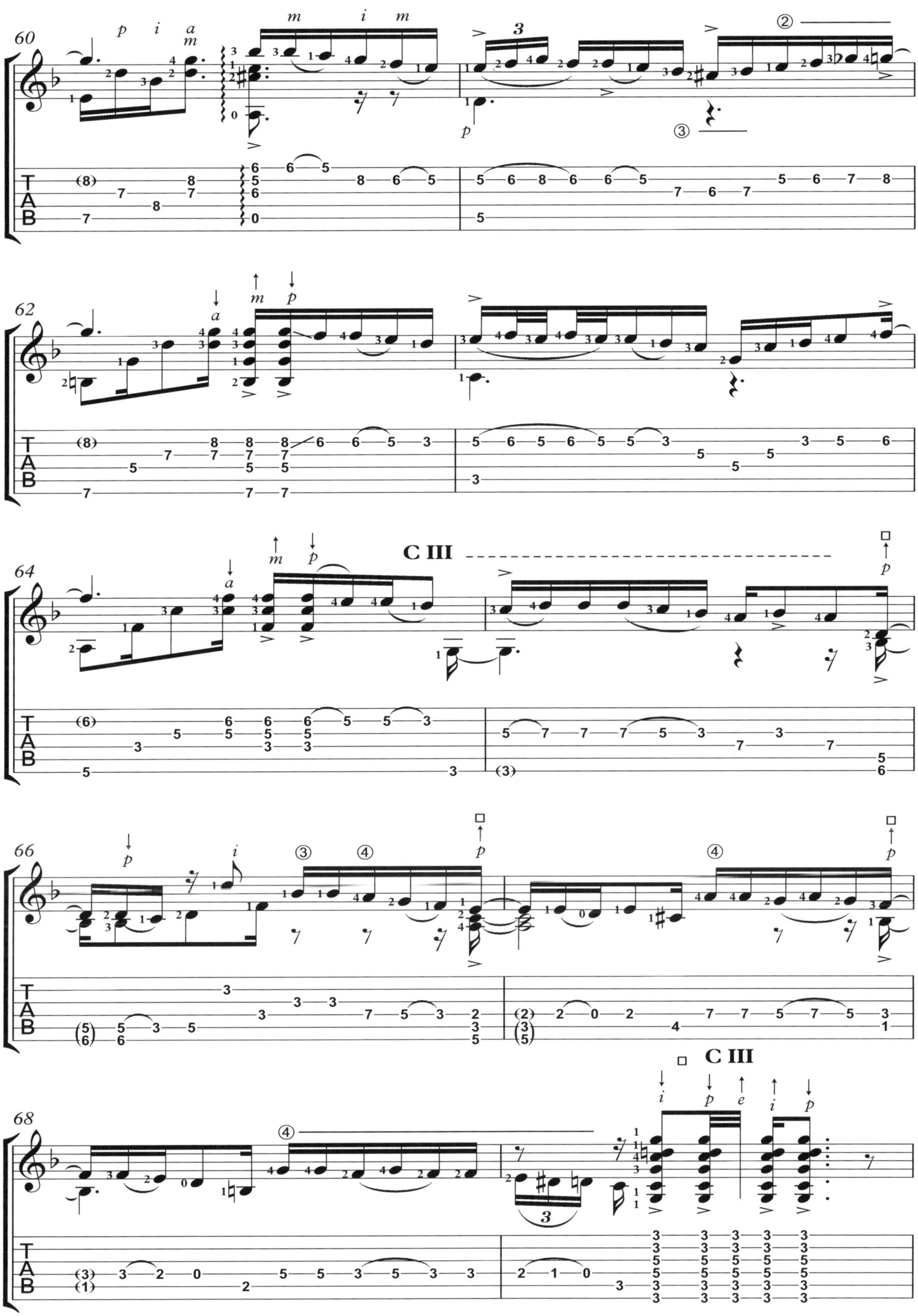
60
62
C III
64
66
68
C III

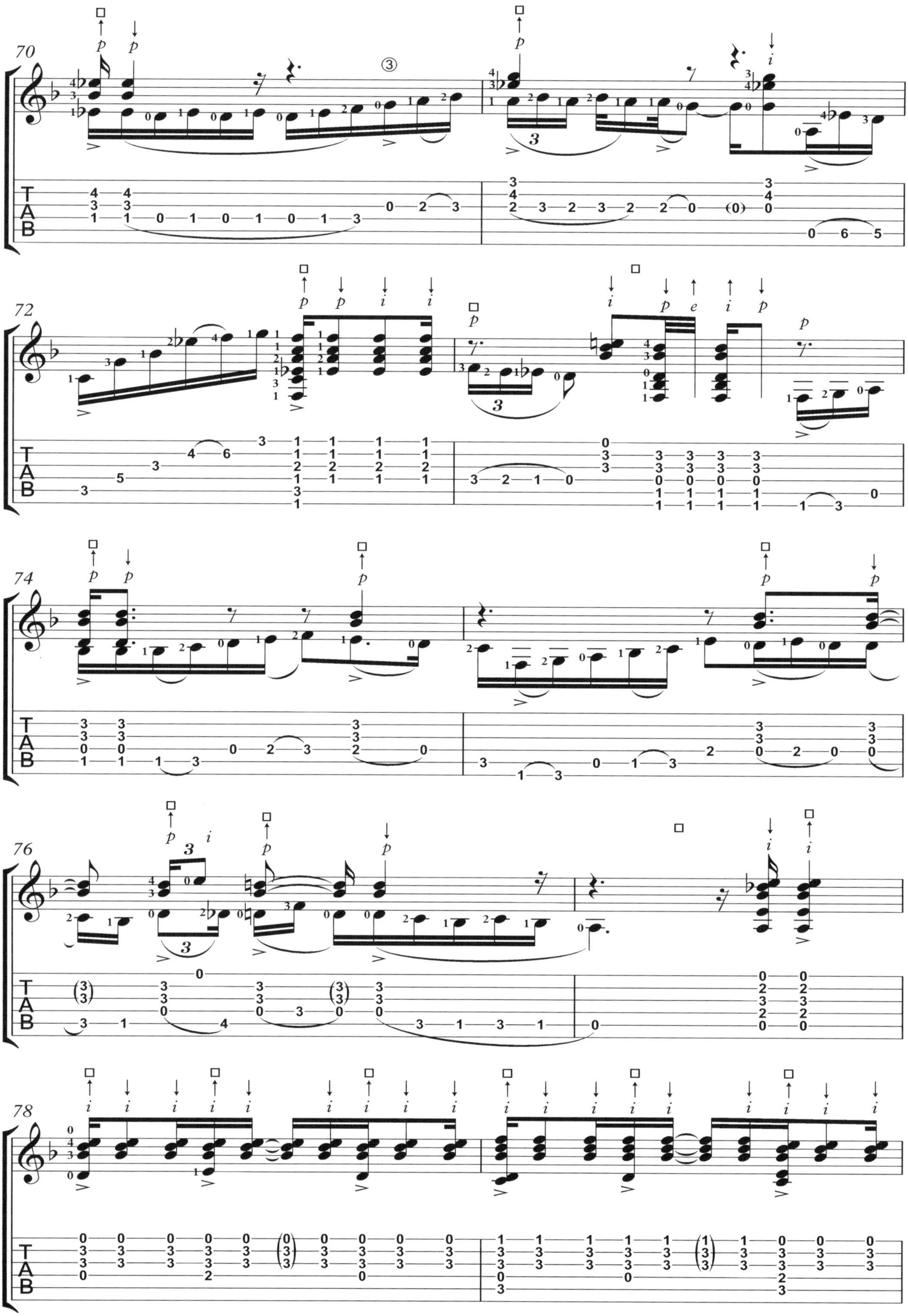

A tempo
mp dolce
leggiero

90
TAB
92
TAB
94
TAB
96
TAB
98
TAB

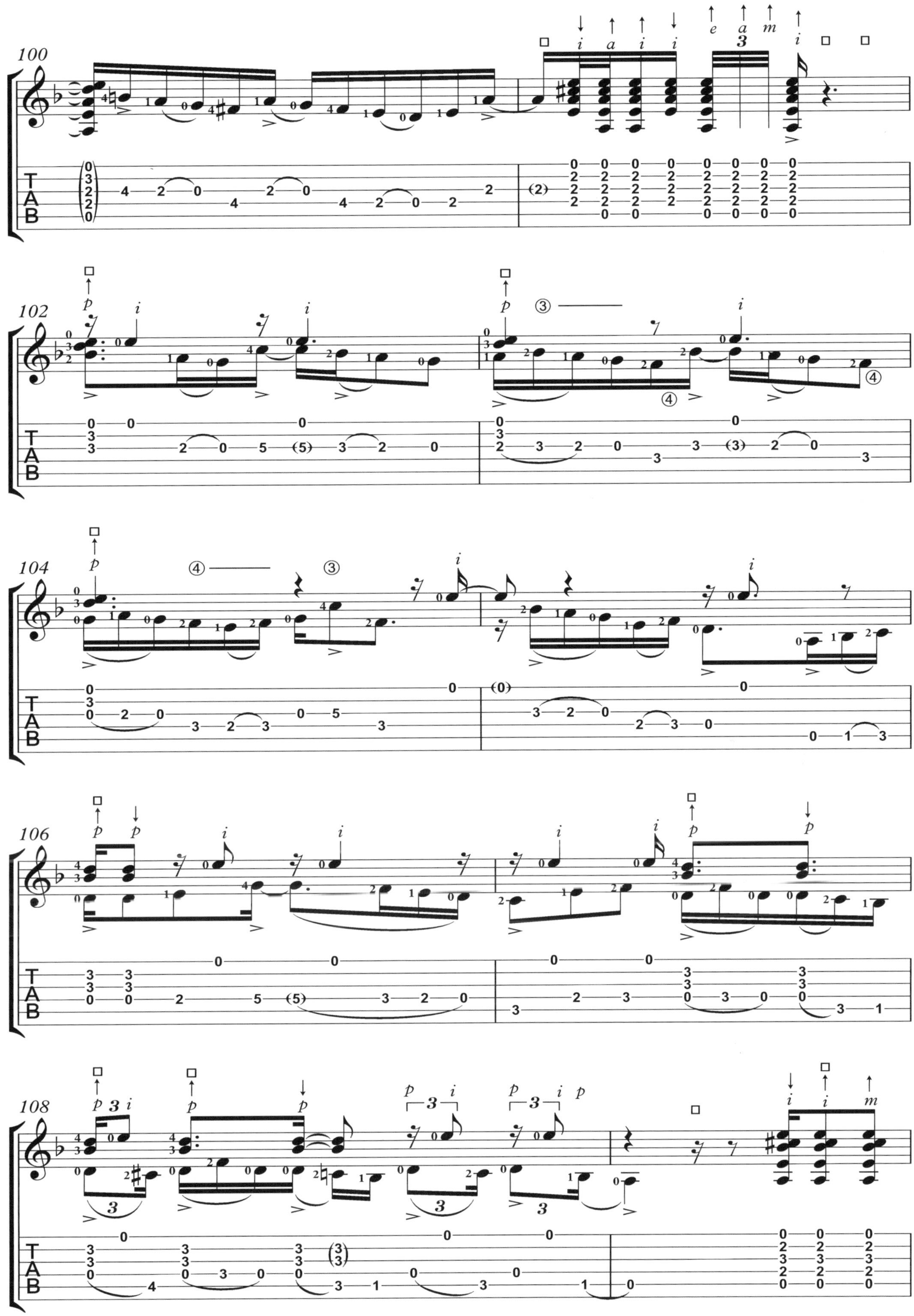
100
102
104
106
108

110
112
114
116
118

120
122
124
126
128
f legato

130
132
CV
134
136
p … sigue
138
TAB

140
142
144
146
148

p … sigue

170
p ....
dim.
172
p i m a p a p a p
174
p i m m
i m i e a m i
i
mf
f
176
p i m a m i
m p p p
mf
p i m a m i
m p p
178
p m p
i i

180
mf
182
184
186
188

190
192
194
196